**This book is dedicated to T'sha & Monty.
You are on my 'thankful' list every day.**

#TheManifestList

"Without true intention and belief, this exercise is futile."

- @SharonEGutierrez

# The Manifest List
## What. Do. You. Want?!

We all have dreams... things we aspire to. Sometimes they lay dormant, asleep and waiting to come to fruition. Other times, they are in front of you, seemingly just out of reach. I spent most of my life expecting the worst, and that became my experience.

Poverty, trauma and abuse were my normal until I decided to reject the victim mentality and work on myself. That is when I learned about something called The Law of Attraction, which is essentially what we focus on, we attract. A few months ago, I was ready to level up. I had a business, but we had recently taken a pretty big hit revenue wise, plus I had moved across the country solo and I found myself stressed, scared and depressed. I was back in the cycle of negativity and had a mindset full of scarcity.

# Manifesting Your Best Life

I was hitting rock bottom again and one day I knew I was done. I reminded myself, I'm not a victim, but powerful and had built from the ground up before and would do it again. I wanted to manifest things I didn't think possible before. I knew there were four things I had to do:

- Know what I wanted to manifest.
- Meditate on it / visualize it.
- Come from a place of gratitude, not desperation or scarcity.
- Take action.

And this is how **The Manifest List** was born. Every single day, I would do the exercise you see in this journal. I started writing down the following: **6 Things To Manifest; 20 Things I'm Thankful For & 3 Action Steps.** A few weeks in, I told my sister about it and she joined in. We lived several thousand miles apart, but she worked for me full time and so we started doing this exercise together over video conference. This truly is an exercise that changed our lives... and I am so honored to be able to share it with you.

Doing this consistently, I've seen some amazing things happen. We've manifested anything from cash to peace of mind to car engines and presents.

Here is what makes it all so powerful:

1. **Writing Things Down:** There is power in our words, whether typed or spoken — but there is something exceedingly powerful in the written word. Not only does it have staying power (a thought can dissolve into nothing, right?) but it focuses us to organize the chaos in our brains.
2. **The Bigger Picture**: In the daily section titled "What Do You Want To Manifest" I want you to write down 6 things you want to bring into your reality. The magic comes in when it is something you truly believe you can achieve, but also are not attached to the "how it will happen". You simply put it out there and release it. Some of my favorite things have been "Feeling Sexy AF", "Peace in the agency" and a "Wall of money and abundance." What do you really want and truly believe you can have?
3. **Thankfulness:** The first 10 things are always easy, but it's the last 10 that you have to get creative. Don't cheat yourself and always put the same things, unless that's what you feel led to do. In the last several months of doing this exercise, I had two big 'aha' moments. First, I noticed that there were more people, and not things, on this list. Isn't it amazing how we can overlook relationships when thinking about gratitude? Second was the fact that I am very thankful for my basic needs

being met. Having a home, a car and health are all things that many, many people go without.
4. **Action:** As much as I wish it were true, you can not create your ideal life by sitting on the couch and visualizing it. You must take action. Each day, you are getting to daydream and look at the big picture. Now you must put energy into making it happen. Look at the things you want to attract in your life, what can you do today to bring them closer to you?

# Your Challenge
## Make This Your Daily Exercise...
## And Change Your Life!

Through the course of this journal, I challenge you to be intentional. Whether you write in it at the same time every day, or just when you feel the need to be grounded, keep coming back and be consistent.

I can't tell you how amazing it is to look back to a week or a month ago and see not only what had transpired but also what actions I had taken to improve my life.

Please tag me, **@SharonEGutierrez**, as you chronicle your journey and use the hashtag **"#TheManifestList"** so we can become a community.

I can't wait to see what you manifest!

Besos,
Sharon Gutierrez

#TheManifestList

Everyone has a dream, a fire, but sometimes we need help igniting that flame. There is a moment when someone is talking about their passion and their purpose. It's in total alignment and you can't help but notice the physical change. You feel lighter, excited and expansive.

What ignites a spark for you?

Date ___/___/___

## The Manifest List
WRITE DOWN SIX THINGS YOU'D LIKE TO MANIFEST IN YOUR LIFE

1. _____
2. _____
3. _____
4. _____
5. _____
6. _____

## Thankful For...
MAKE A LIST OF 20 THINGS YOU ARE THANKFUL FOR TODAY

## Take Action
WHAT ARE 3 THINGS YOU CAN DO TO MOVE THINGS FORWARD?

1. _____
2. _____
3. _____

Date ___/___/___

## The Manifest List
WRITE DOWN SIX THINGS YOU'D LIKE TO MANIFEST IN YOUR LIFE

1. _____
2. _____
3. _____
4. _____
5. _____
6. _____

## Thankful For...
MAKE A LIST OF 20 THINGS YOU ARE THANKFUL FOR TODAY




## Take Action
WHAT ARE 3 THINGS YOU CAN DO TO MOVE THINGS FORWARD?

1. _____
2. _____
3. _____

Date    /    /

# The Manifest List
WRITE DOWN SIX THINGS YOU'D LIKE TO MANIFEST IN YOUR LIFE

1. _____
2. _____
3. _____
4. _____
5. _____
6. _____

# Thankful For...
MAKE A LIST OF 20 THINGS YOU ARE THANKFUL FOR TODAY




# Take Action
WHAT ARE 3 THINGS YOU CAN DO TO MOVE THINGS FORWARD?

1. _____
2. _____
3. _____

Date ___ / ___ / ___

## The Manifest List
WRITE DOWN SIX THINGS YOU'D LIKE TO MANIFEST IN YOUR LIFE

1. _____
2. _____
3. _____
4. _____
5. _____
6. _____

## Thankful For...
MAKE A LIST OF 20 THINGS YOU ARE THANKFUL FOR TODAY




## Take Action
WHAT ARE 3 THINGS YOU CAN DO TO MOVE THINGS FORWARD?

1. _____
2. _____
3. _____

Date     /     /

# The Manifest List
WRITE DOWN SIX THINGS YOU'D LIKE TO MANIFEST IN YOUR LIFE

1. _____
2. _____
3. _____
4. _____
5. _____
6. _____

# Thankful For...
MAKE A LIST OF 20 THINGS YOU ARE THANKFUL FOR TODAY




# Take Action
WHAT ARE 3 THINGS YOU CAN DO TO MOVE THINGS FORWARD?

1. _____
2. _____
3. _____

Date    /    /

# The Manifest List
WRITE DOWN SIX THINGS YOU'D LIKE TO MANIFEST IN YOUR LIFE

1. _____
2. _____
3. _____
4. _____
5. _____
6. _____

# Thankful For...
MAKE A LIST OF 20 THINGS YOU ARE THANKFUL FOR TODAY

# Take Action
WHAT ARE 3 THINGS YOU CAN DO TO MOVE THINGS FORWARD?

1. _____
2. _____
3. _____

Date    /    /

## The Manifest List
WRITE DOWN SIX THINGS YOU'D LIKE TO MANIFEST IN YOUR LIFE

1. _____
2. _____
3. _____
4. _____
5. _____
6. _____

## Thankful For...
MAKE A LIST OF 20 THINGS YOU ARE THANKFUL FOR TODAY

## Take Action
WHAT ARE 3 THINGS YOU CAN DO TO MOVE THINGS FORWARD?

1. _____
2. _____
3. _____

Date     /     /

# The Manifest List
WRITE DOWN SIX THINGS YOU'D LIKE TO MANIFEST IN YOUR LIFE

1. _____
2. _____
3. _____
4. _____
5. _____
6. _____

# Thankful For...
MAKE A LIST OF 20 THINGS YOU ARE THANKFUL FOR TODAY

# Take Action
WHAT ARE 3 THINGS YOU CAN DO TO MOVE THINGS FORWARD?

1. _____
2. _____
3. _____

Date ___ / ___ / ___

# The Manifest List
WRITE DOWN SIX THINGS YOU'D LIKE TO MANIFEST IN YOUR LIFE

1. _____
2. _____
3. _____
4. _____
5. _____
6. _____

# Thankful For...
MAKE A LIST OF 20 THINGS YOU ARE THANKFUL FOR TODAY




# Take Action
WHAT ARE 3 THINGS YOU CAN DO TO MOVE THINGS FORWARD?

1. _____
2. _____
3. _____

Date     /    /

# The Manifest List
WRITE DOWN SIX THINGS YOU'D LIKE TO MANIFEST IN YOUR LIFE

1. _____
2. _____
3. _____
4. _____
5. _____
6. _____

# Thankful For...
MAKE A LIST OF 20 THINGS YOU ARE THANKFUL FOR TODAY




# Take Action
WHAT ARE 3 THINGS YOU CAN DO TO MOVE THINGS FORWARD?

1. _____
2. _____
3. _____

Date     /     /

# Reflections

#TheManifestList

#TheManifestList

**Abundance is not something we acquire, it is something we tune into.**

- Wayne Dyer

Date     /     /

# The Manifest List
**WRITE DOWN SIX THINGS YOU'D LIKE TO MANIFEST IN YOUR LIFE**

1. _____
2. _____
3. _____
4. _____
5. _____
6. _____

# Thankful For...
**MAKE A LIST OF 20 THINGS YOU ARE THANKFUL FOR TODAY**




# Take Action
**WHAT ARE 3 THINGS YOU CAN DO TO MOVE THINGS FORWARD?**

1. _____
2. _____
3. _____

Date    /    /

## The Manifest List
WRITE DOWN SIX THINGS YOU'D LIKE TO MANIFEST IN YOUR LIFE

1. _____
2. _____
3. _____
4. _____
5. _____
6. _____

## Thankful For...
MAKE A LIST OF 20 THINGS YOU ARE THANKFUL FOR TODAY




## Take Action
WHAT ARE 3 THINGS YOU CAN DO TO MOVE THINGS FORWARD?

1. _____
2. _____
3. _____

Date      /    /

# The Manifest List
WRITE DOWN SIX THINGS YOU'D LIKE TO MANIFEST IN YOUR LIFE

1. _____
2. _____
3. _____
4. _____
5. _____
6. _____

# Thankful For...
MAKE A LIST OF 20 THINGS YOU ARE THANKFUL FOR TODAY




# Take Action
WHAT ARE 3 THINGS YOU CAN DO TO MOVE THINGS FORWARD?

1. _____
2. _____
3. _____

Date     /     /

# The Manifest List
WRITE DOWN SIX THINGS YOU'D LIKE TO MANIFEST IN YOUR LIFE

1. _____
2. _____
3. _____
4. _____
5. _____
6. _____

# Thankful For...
MAKE A LIST OF 20 THINGS YOU ARE THANKFUL FOR TODAY




# Take Action
WHAT ARE 3 THINGS YOU CAN DO TO MOVE THINGS FORWARD?

1. _____
2. _____
3. _____

Date     /     /

## The Manifest List
WRITE DOWN SIX THINGS YOU'D LIKE TO MANIFEST IN YOUR LIFE

1. _____
2. _____
3. _____
4. _____
5. _____
6. _____

## Thankful For...
MAKE A LIST OF 20 THINGS YOU ARE THANKFUL FOR TODAY




## Take Action
WHAT ARE 3 THINGS YOU CAN DO TO MOVE THINGS FORWARD?

1. _____
2. _____
3. _____

Date     /     /

## The Manifest List
WRITE DOWN SIX THINGS YOU'D LIKE TO MANIFEST IN YOUR LIFE

1. _____
2. _____
3. _____
4. _____
5. _____
6. _____

## Thankful For...
MAKE A LIST OF 20 THINGS YOU ARE THANKFUL FOR TODAY

## Take Action
WHAT ARE 3 THINGS YOU CAN DO TO MOVE THINGS FORWARD?

1. _____
2. _____
3. _____

Date      /    /

# The Manifest List
WRITE DOWN SIX THINGS YOU'D LIKE TO MANIFEST IN YOUR LIFE

1. _____
2. _____
3. _____
4. _____
5. _____
6. _____

# Thankful For...
MAKE A LIST OF 20 THINGS YOU ARE THANKFUL FOR TODAY




# Take Action
WHAT ARE 3 THINGS YOU CAN DO TO MOVE THINGS FORWARD?

1. _____
2. _____
3. _____

Date    /    /

## The Manifest List
WRITE DOWN SIX THINGS YOU'D LIKE TO MANIFEST IN YOUR LIFE

1. _____
2. _____
3. _____
4. _____
5. _____
6. _____

## Thankful For...
MAKE A LIST OF 20 THINGS YOU ARE THANKFUL FOR TODAY




## Take Action
WHAT ARE 3 THINGS YOU CAN DO TO MOVE THINGS FORWARD?

1. _____
2. _____
3. _____

Date ___/___/___

# The Manifest List
WRITE DOWN SIX THINGS YOU'D LIKE TO MANIFEST IN YOUR LIFE

1. _____
2. _____
3. _____
4. _____
5. _____
6. _____

# Thankful For...
MAKE A LIST OF 20 THINGS YOU ARE THANKFUL FOR TODAY

# Take Action
WHAT ARE 3 THINGS YOU CAN DO TO MOVE THINGS FORWARD?

1. _____
2. _____
3. _____

Date    /    /

# The Manifest List
WRITE DOWN SIX THINGS YOU'D LIKE TO MANIFEST IN YOUR LIFE

1. _____
2. _____
3. _____
4. _____
5. _____
6. _____

# Thankful For...
MAKE A LIST OF 20 THINGS YOU ARE THANKFUL FOR TODAY




# Take Action
WHAT ARE 3 THINGS YOU CAN DO TO MOVE THINGS FORWARD?

1. _____
2. _____
3. _____

Date     /     /

# Reflections

#TheManifestList

#TheManifestList

"Everything you want is out there waiting for you to ask. Everything you want also wants you. But you have to take action to get it."

- Jack Canfield

Date    /    /

# The Manifest List
WRITE DOWN SIX THINGS YOU'D LIKE TO MANIFEST IN YOUR LIFE

1. _____
2. _____
3. _____
4. _____
5. _____
6. _____

# Thankful For...
MAKE A LIST OF 20 THINGS YOU ARE THANKFUL FOR TODAY




# Take Action
WHAT ARE 3 THINGS YOU CAN DO TO MOVE THINGS FORWARD?

1. _____
2. _____
3. _____

Date        /      /

# The Manifest List
WRITE DOWN SIX THINGS YOU'D LIKE TO MANIFEST IN YOUR LIFE

1. _____
2. _____
3. _____
4. _____
5. _____
6. _____

# Thankful For...
MAKE A LIST OF 20 THINGS YOU ARE THANKFUL FOR TODAY

# Take Action
WHAT ARE 3 THINGS YOU CAN DO TO MOVE THINGS FORWARD?

1. _____
2. _____
3. _____

Date    /    /

# The Manifest List
WRITE DOWN SIX THINGS YOU'D LIKE TO MANIFEST IN YOUR LIFE

1. _____
2. _____
3. _____
4. _____
5. _____
6. _____

# Thankful For...
MAKE A LIST OF 20 THINGS YOU ARE THANKFUL FOR TODAY




# Take Action
**WHAT ARE 3 THINGS YOU CAN DO TO MOVE THINGS FORWARD?**

1. _____
2. _____
3. _____

Date    /    /

# The Manifest List
WRITE DOWN SIX THINGS YOU'D LIKE TO MANIFEST IN YOUR LIFE

1. _____
2. _____
3. _____
4. _____
5. _____
6. _____

# Thankful For...
MAKE A LIST OF 20 THINGS YOU ARE THANKFUL FOR TODAY




# Take Action
WHAT ARE 3 THINGS YOU CAN DO TO MOVE THINGS FORWARD?

1. _____
2. _____
3. _____

Date ___ / ___ / ___

# The Manifest List
WRITE DOWN SIX THINGS YOU'D LIKE TO MANIFEST IN YOUR LIFE

1. _____
2. _____
3. _____
4. _____
5. _____
6. _____

# Thankful For...
MAKE A LIST OF 20 THINGS YOU ARE THANKFUL FOR TODAY

# Take Action
WHAT ARE 3 THINGS YOU CAN DO TO MOVE THINGS FORWARD?

1. _____
2. _____
3. _____

Date    /    /

## The Manifest List
WRITE DOWN SIX THINGS YOU'D LIKE TO MANIFEST IN YOUR LIFE

1. _____
2. _____
3. _____
4. _____
5. _____
6. _____

## Thankful For...
MAKE A LIST OF 20 THINGS YOU ARE THANKFUL FOR TODAY




## Take Action
WHAT ARE 3 THINGS YOU CAN DO TO MOVE THINGS FORWARD?

1. _____
2. _____
3. _____

Date      /    /

# The Manifest List
WRITE DOWN SIX THINGS YOU'D LIKE TO MANIFEST IN YOUR LIFE

1. _____
2. _____
3. _____
4. _____
5. _____
6. _____

# Thankful For...
MAKE A LIST OF 20 THINGS YOU ARE THANKFUL FOR TODAY

# Take Action
WHAT ARE 3 THINGS YOU CAN DO TO MOVE THINGS FORWARD?

1. _____
2. _____
3. _____

Date     /     /

## The Manifest List
WRITE DOWN SIX THINGS YOU'D LIKE TO MANIFEST IN YOUR LIFE

1. _____
2. _____
3. _____
4. _____
5. _____
6. _____

## Thankful For...
MAKE A LIST OF 20 THINGS YOU ARE THANKFUL FOR TODAY

## Take Action
WHAT ARE 3 THINGS YOU CAN DO TO MOVE THINGS FORWARD?

1. _____
2. _____
3. _____

Date ___/___/___

# The Manifest List
WRITE DOWN SIX THINGS YOU'D LIKE TO MANIFEST IN YOUR LIFE

1. _____
2. _____
3. _____
4. _____
5. _____
6. _____

# Thankful For...
MAKE A LIST OF 20 THINGS YOU ARE THANKFUL FOR TODAY

# Take Action
WHAT ARE 3 THINGS YOU CAN DO TO MOVE THINGS FORWARD?

1. _____
2. _____
3. _____

Date     /     /

## The Manifest List
WRITE DOWN SIX THINGS YOU'D LIKE TO MANIFEST IN YOUR LIFE

1. _____
2. _____
3. _____
4. _____
5. _____
6. _____

## Thankful For...
MAKE A LIST OF 20 THINGS YOU ARE THANKFUL FOR TODAY




## Take Action
WHAT ARE 3 THINGS YOU CAN DO TO MOVE THINGS FORWARD?

1. _____
2. _____
3. _____

Date / /

# Reflections

#TheManifestList

#TheManifestList

"Never. Stop. Events may have been put into momentum moments, days, weeks or years ago. A conversation on a subway may have changed the course of your entire future because you were introduced to a new idea. Trust the process and continue forward."

- @SharonEGutierrez

Date ___ / ___ / ___

## The Manifest List
WRITE DOWN SIX THINGS YOU'D LIKE TO MANIFEST IN YOUR LIFE

1. _____
2. _____
3. _____
4. _____
5. _____
6. _____

## Thankful For...
MAKE A LIST OF 20 THINGS YOU ARE THANKFUL FOR TODAY




## Take Action
WHAT ARE 3 THINGS YOU CAN DO TO MOVE THINGS FORWARD?

1. _____
2. _____
3. _____

Date    /    /

## The Manifest List
WRITE DOWN SIX THINGS YOU'D LIKE TO MANIFEST IN YOUR LIFE

1. _____
2. _____
3. _____
4. _____
5. _____
6. _____

## Thankful For...
MAKE A LIST OF 20 THINGS YOU ARE THANKFUL FOR TODAY

## Take Action
WHAT ARE 3 THINGS YOU CAN DO TO MOVE THINGS FORWARD?

1. _____
2. _____
3. _____

Date    /    /

# The Manifest List
WRITE DOWN SIX THINGS YOU'D LIKE TO MANIFEST IN YOUR LIFE

1. _____
2. _____
3. _____
4. _____
5. _____
6. _____

# Thankful For...
MAKE A LIST OF 20 THINGS YOU ARE THANKFUL FOR TODAY




# Take Action
WHAT ARE 3 THINGS YOU CAN DO TO MOVE THINGS FORWARD?

1. _____
2. _____
3. _____

Date    /    /

## The Manifest List
WRITE DOWN SIX THINGS YOU'D LIKE TO MANIFEST IN YOUR LIFE

1. _____
2. _____
3. _____
4. _____
5. _____
6. _____

## Thankful For...
MAKE A LIST OF 20 THINGS YOU ARE THANKFUL FOR TODAY




## Take Action
WHAT ARE 3 THINGS YOU CAN DO TO MOVE THINGS FORWARD?

1. _____
2. _____
3. _____

Date ___ / ___ / ___

## The Manifest List
WRITE DOWN SIX THINGS YOU'D LIKE TO MANIFEST IN YOUR LIFE

1. _____
2. _____
3. _____
4. _____
5. _____
6. _____

## Thankful For...
MAKE A LIST OF 20 THINGS YOU ARE THANKFUL FOR TODAY

## Take Action
WHAT ARE 3 THINGS YOU CAN DO TO MOVE THINGS FORWARD?

1. _____
2. _____
3. _____

Date     /     /

# The Manifest List
WRITE DOWN SIX THINGS YOU'D LIKE TO MANIFEST IN YOUR LIFE

1. _____
2. _____
3. _____
4. _____
5. _____
6. _____

# Thankful For...
MAKE A LIST OF 20 THINGS YOU ARE THANKFUL FOR TODAY

# Take Action
WHAT ARE 3 THINGS YOU CAN DO TO MOVE THINGS FORWARD?

1. _____
2. _____
3. _____

Date     /   /

# The Manifest List
WRITE DOWN SIX THINGS YOU'D LIKE TO MANIFEST IN YOUR LIFE

1. _____
2. _____
3. _____
4. _____
5. _____
6. _____

# Thankful For...
MAKE A LIST OF 20 THINGS YOU ARE THANKFUL FOR TODAY




# Take Action
WHAT ARE 3 THINGS YOU CAN DO TO MOVE THINGS FORWARD?

1. _____
2. _____
3. _____

Date     /     /

# The Manifest List
WRITE DOWN SIX THINGS YOU'D LIKE TO MANIFEST IN YOUR LIFE

1. _____
2. _____
3. _____
4. _____
5. _____
6. _____

# Thankful For...
MAKE A LIST OF 20 THINGS YOU ARE THANKFUL FOR TODAY




# Take Action
WHAT ARE 3 THINGS YOU CAN DO TO MOVE THINGS FORWARD?

1. _____
2. _____
3. _____

Date ___ / ___ / ___

## The Manifest List
WRITE DOWN SIX THINGS YOU'D LIKE TO MANIFEST IN YOUR LIFE

1. _____
2. _____
3. _____
4. _____
5. _____
6. _____

## Thankful For...
MAKE A LIST OF 20 THINGS YOU ARE THANKFUL FOR TODAY




## Take Action
WHAT ARE 3 THINGS YOU CAN DO TO MOVE THINGS FORWARD?

1. _____
2. _____
3. _____

Date     /    /

# The Manifest List
WRITE DOWN SIX THINGS YOU'D LIKE TO MANIFEST IN YOUR LIFE

1. _____
2. _____
3. _____
4. _____
5. _____
6. _____

# Thankful For...
MAKE A LIST OF 20 THINGS YOU ARE THANKFUL FOR TODAY




# Take Action
WHAT ARE 3 THINGS YOU CAN DO TO MOVE THINGS FORWARD?

1. _____
2. _____
3. _____

Date    /    /

# Reflections

#TheManifestList

#TheManifestList

"Have It All: You can have it all, you just have to decide what it 'all' means to you!"

- @DrRupaWong

Date ___ / ___ / ___

# The Manifest List
WRITE DOWN SIX THINGS YOU'D LIKE TO MANIFEST IN YOUR LIFE

1. _____
2. _____
3. _____
4. _____
5. _____
6. _____

# Thankful For...
MAKE A LIST OF 20 THINGS YOU ARE THANKFUL FOR TODAY




# Take Action
WHAT ARE 3 THINGS YOU CAN DO TO MOVE THINGS FORWARD?

1. _____
2. _____
3. _____

Date     /     /

# The Manifest List
WRITE DOWN SIX THINGS YOU'D LIKE TO MANIFEST IN YOUR LIFE

1. _____
2. _____
3. _____
4. _____
5. _____
6. _____

# Thankful For...
MAKE A LIST OF 20 THINGS YOU ARE THANKFUL FOR TODAY

# Take Action
WHAT ARE 3 THINGS YOU CAN DO TO MOVE THINGS FORWARD?

1. _____
2. _____
3. _____

Date     /     /

# The Manifest List
WRITE DOWN SIX THINGS YOU'D LIKE TO MANIFEST IN YOUR LIFE

1. _____
2. _____
3. _____
4. _____
5. _____
6. _____

# Thankful For...
MAKE A LIST OF 20 THINGS YOU ARE THANKFUL FOR TODAY




# Take Action
WHAT ARE 3 THINGS YOU CAN DO TO MOVE THINGS FORWARD?

1. _____
2. _____
3. _____

Date    /    /

## The Manifest List
WRITE DOWN SIX THINGS YOU'D LIKE TO MANIFEST IN YOUR LIFE

1. _____
2. _____
3. _____
4. _____
5. _____
6. _____

## Thankful For...
MAKE A LIST OF 20 THINGS YOU ARE THANKFUL FOR TODAY




## Take Action
WHAT ARE 3 THINGS YOU CAN DO TO MOVE THINGS FORWARD?

1. _____
2. _____
3. _____

Date    /    /

# The Manifest List
WRITE DOWN SIX THINGS YOU'D LIKE TO MANIFEST IN YOUR LIFE

1. _____
2. _____
3. _____
4. _____
5. _____
6. _____

# Thankful For...
MAKE A LIST OF 20 THINGS YOU ARE THANKFUL FOR TODAY




# Take Action
WHAT ARE 3 THINGS YOU CAN DO TO MOVE THINGS FORWARD?

1. _____
2. _____
3. _____

Date    /    /

# The Manifest List
WRITE DOWN SIX THINGS YOU'D LIKE TO MANIFEST IN YOUR LIFE

1. _____
2. _____
3. _____
4. _____
5. _____
6. _____

# Thankful For...
MAKE A LIST OF 20 THINGS YOU ARE THANKFUL FOR TODAY




# Take Action
WHAT ARE 3 THINGS YOU CAN DO TO MOVE THINGS FORWARD?

1. _____
2. _____
3. _____

Date ___/___/___

# The Manifest List
WRITE DOWN SIX THINGS YOU'D LIKE TO MANIFEST IN YOUR LIFE

1. _____
2. _____
3. _____
4. _____
5. _____
6. _____

# Thankful For...
MAKE A LIST OF 20 THINGS YOU ARE THANKFUL FOR TODAY




# Take Action
WHAT ARE 3 THINGS YOU CAN DO TO MOVE THINGS FORWARD?

1. _____
2. _____
3. _____

Date    /    /

# The Manifest List
WRITE DOWN SIX THINGS YOU'D LIKE TO MANIFEST IN YOUR LIFE

1. _____
2. _____
3. _____
4. _____
5. _____
6. _____

# Thankful For...
MAKE A LIST OF 20 THINGS YOU ARE THANKFUL FOR TODAY




# Take Action
WHAT ARE 3 THINGS YOU CAN DO TO MOVE THINGS FORWARD?

1. _____
2. _____
3. _____

Date     /     /

## The Manifest List
WRITE DOWN SIX THINGS YOU'D LIKE TO MANIFEST IN YOUR LIFE

1. _____
2. _____
3. _____
4. _____
5. _____
6. _____

## Thankful For...
MAKE A LIST OF 20 THINGS YOU ARE THANKFUL FOR TODAY




## Take Action
WHAT ARE 3 THINGS YOU CAN DO TO MOVE THINGS FORWARD?

1. _____
2. _____
3. _____

Date    /    /

# The Manifest List
WRITE DOWN SIX THINGS YOU'D LIKE TO MANIFEST IN YOUR LIFE

1. _____
2. _____
3. _____
4. _____
5. _____
6. _____

# Thankful For...
MAKE A LIST OF 20 THINGS YOU ARE THANKFUL FOR TODAY




# Take Action
WHAT ARE 3 THINGS YOU CAN DO TO MOVE THINGS FORWARD?

1. _____
2. _____
3. _____

Date    /    /

# Reflections

#TheManifestList

#TheManifestList

"It's so powerful when you stop and choose to be thankful.

When you are thankful, really genuinely appreciative for what you have, big or small, it creates space and appreciation for all the new things that come into your life."

- @SharonEGutierrez & @TshaGutierrez

Date ___/___/___

## The Manifest List
WRITE DOWN SIX THINGS YOU'D LIKE TO MANIFEST IN YOUR LIFE

1. _____
2. _____
3. _____
4. _____
5. _____
6. _____

## Thankful For...
MAKE A LIST OF 20 THINGS YOU ARE THANKFUL FOR TODAY




## Take Action
WHAT ARE 3 THINGS YOU CAN DO TO MOVE THINGS FORWARD?

1. _____
2. _____
3. _____

Date    /    /

## The Manifest List
WRITE DOWN SIX THINGS YOU'D LIKE TO MANIFEST IN YOUR LIFE

1. _____
2. _____
3. _____
4. _____
5. _____
6. _____

## Thankful For...
MAKE A LIST OF 20 THINGS YOU ARE THANKFUL FOR TODAY

## Take Action
WHAT ARE 3 THINGS YOU CAN DO TO MOVE THINGS FORWARD?

1. _____
2. _____
3. _____

Date     /    /

# The Manifest List
WRITE DOWN SIX THINGS YOU'D LIKE TO MANIFEST IN YOUR LIFE

1. _____
2. _____
3. _____
4. _____
5. _____
6. _____

# Thankful For...
MAKE A LIST OF 20 THINGS YOU ARE THANKFUL FOR TODAY




# Take Action
WHAT ARE 3 THINGS YOU CAN DO TO MOVE THINGS FORWARD?

1. _____
2. _____
3. _____

Date     /    /

# The Manifest List
WRITE DOWN SIX THINGS YOU'D LIKE TO MANIFEST IN YOUR LIFE

1. _____
2. _____
3. _____
4. _____
5. _____
6. _____

# Thankful For...
MAKE A LIST OF 20 THINGS YOU ARE THANKFUL FOR TODAY

# Take Action
WHAT ARE 3 THINGS YOU CAN DO TO MOVE THINGS FORWARD?

1. _____
2. _____
3. _____

Date ___/___/___

# The Manifest List
WRITE DOWN SIX THINGS YOU'D LIKE TO MANIFEST IN YOUR LIFE

1. _____
2. _____
3. _____
4. _____
5. _____
6. _____

# Thankful For...
MAKE A LIST OF 20 THINGS YOU ARE THANKFUL FOR TODAY




# Take Action
WHAT ARE 3 THINGS YOU CAN DO TO MOVE THINGS FORWARD?

1. _____
2. _____
3. _____

Date    /    /

## The Manifest List
WRITE DOWN SIX THINGS YOU'D LIKE TO MANIFEST IN YOUR LIFE

1. _____
2. _____
3. _____
4. _____
5. _____
6. _____

## Thankful For...
MAKE A LIST OF 20 THINGS YOU ARE THANKFUL FOR TODAY

## Take Action
WHAT ARE 3 THINGS YOU CAN DO TO MOVE THINGS FORWARD?

1. _____
2. _____
3. _____

Date     /     /

# The Manifest List
WRITE DOWN SIX THINGS YOU'D LIKE TO MANIFEST IN YOUR LIFE

1. _____
2. _____
3. _____
4. _____
5. _____
6. _____

# Thankful For...
MAKE A LIST OF 20 THINGS YOU ARE THANKFUL FOR TODAY




# Take Action
**WHAT ARE 3 THINGS YOU CAN DO TO MOVE THINGS FORWARD?**

1. _____
2. _____
3. _____

Date    /    /

## The Manifest List
WRITE DOWN SIX THINGS YOU'D LIKE TO MANIFEST IN YOUR LIFE

1. _____
2. _____
3. _____
4. _____
5. _____
6. _____

## Thankful For...
MAKE A LIST OF 20 THINGS YOU ARE THANKFUL FOR TODAY

## Take Action
WHAT ARE 3 THINGS YOU CAN DO TO MOVE THINGS FORWARD?

1. _____
2. _____
3. _____

Date ___ / ___ / ___

## The Manifest List
WRITE DOWN SIX THINGS YOU'D LIKE TO MANIFEST IN YOUR LIFE

1. _____
2. _____
3. _____
4. _____
5. _____
6. _____

## Thankful For...
MAKE A LIST OF 20 THINGS YOU ARE THANKFUL FOR TODAY

## Take Action
WHAT ARE 3 THINGS YOU CAN DO TO MOVE THINGS FORWARD?

1. _____
2. _____
3. _____

Date    /    /

# The Manifest List
WRITE DOWN SIX THINGS YOU'D LIKE TO MANIFEST IN YOUR LIFE

1. _____
2. _____
3. _____
4. _____
5. _____
6. _____

# Thankful For...
MAKE A LIST OF 20 THINGS YOU ARE THANKFUL FOR TODAY

# Take Action
WHAT ARE 3 THINGS YOU CAN DO TO MOVE THINGS FORWARD?

1. _____
2. _____
3. _____

Date     /   /

# Reflections

#TheManifestList

#TheManifestList

"The time has come for you to stop procrastinating and step out in faith to be all that God has called for you to be. With persistence and consistent pursuit, the manifestation of your dreams can be turned into your reality."

- @RiaCNewbold

Date     /    /

## The Manifest List
WRITE DOWN SIX THINGS YOU'D LIKE TO MANIFEST IN YOUR LIFE

1. _____
2. _____
3. _____
4. _____
5. _____
6. _____

## Thankful For...
MAKE A LIST OF 20 THINGS YOU ARE THANKFUL FOR TODAY




## Take Action
WHAT ARE 3 THINGS YOU CAN DO TO MOVE THINGS FORWARD?

1. _____
2. _____
3. _____

Date    /    /

# The Manifest List
WRITE DOWN SIX THINGS YOU'D LIKE TO MANIFEST IN YOUR LIFE

1. _____
2. _____
3. _____
4. _____
5. _____
6. _____

# Thankful For...
MAKE A LIST OF 20 THINGS YOU ARE THANKFUL FOR TODAY




# Take Action
WHAT ARE 3 THINGS YOU CAN DO TO MOVE THINGS FORWARD?

1. _____
2. _____
3. _____

Date ___/___/___

# The Manifest List
WRITE DOWN SIX THINGS YOU'D LIKE TO MANIFEST IN YOUR LIFE

1. _____
2. _____
3. _____
4. _____
5. _____
6. _____

# Thankful For...
MAKE A LIST OF 20 THINGS YOU ARE THANKFUL FOR TODAY




# Take Action
WHAT ARE 3 THINGS YOU CAN DO TO MOVE THINGS FORWARD?

1. _____
2. _____
3. _____

Date ___ / ___ / ___

## The Manifest List
WRITE DOWN SIX THINGS YOU'D LIKE TO MANIFEST IN YOUR LIFE

1. _____
2. _____
3. _____
4. _____
5. _____
6. _____

## Thankful For...
MAKE A LIST OF 20 THINGS YOU ARE THANKFUL FOR TODAY

## Take Action
WHAT ARE 3 THINGS YOU CAN DO TO MOVE THINGS FORWARD?

1. _____
2. _____
3. _____

Date ___/___/___

# The Manifest List
WRITE DOWN SIX THINGS YOU'D LIKE TO MANIFEST IN YOUR LIFE

1. _____
2. _____
3. _____
4. _____
5. _____
6. _____

# Thankful For...
MAKE A LIST OF 20 THINGS YOU ARE THANKFUL FOR TODAY




# Take Action
WHAT ARE 3 THINGS YOU CAN DO TO MOVE THINGS FORWARD?

1. _____
2. _____
3. _____

Date ___ / ___ / ___

# The Manifest List
WRITE DOWN SIX THINGS YOU'D LIKE TO MANIFEST IN YOUR LIFE

1. _____
2. _____
3. _____
4. _____
5. _____
6. _____

# Thankful For...
MAKE A LIST OF 20 THINGS YOU ARE THANKFUL FOR TODAY

# Take Action
WHAT ARE 3 THINGS YOU CAN DO TO MOVE THINGS FORWARD?

1. _____
2. _____
3. _____

Date ___ / ___ / ___

# The Manifest List
WRITE DOWN SIX THINGS YOU'D LIKE TO MANIFEST IN YOUR LIFE

1. _____
2. _____
3. _____
4. _____
5. _____
6. _____

# Thankful For...
**MAKE A LIST OF 20 THINGS YOU ARE THANKFUL FOR TODAY**

# Take Action
**WHAT ARE 3 THINGS YOU CAN DO TO MOVE THINGS FORWARD?**

1. _____
2. _____
3. _____

Date    /    /

## The Manifest List
WRITE DOWN SIX THINGS YOU'D LIKE TO MANIFEST IN YOUR LIFE

1. _____
2. _____
3. _____
4. _____
5. _____
6. _____

## Thankful For...
MAKE A LIST OF 20 THINGS YOU ARE THANKFUL FOR TODAY




## Take Action
WHAT ARE 3 THINGS YOU CAN DO TO MOVE THINGS FORWARD?

1. _____
2. _____
3. _____

Date    /    /

# The Manifest List
WRITE DOWN SIX THINGS YOU'D LIKE TO MANIFEST IN YOUR LIFE

1. _____
2. _____
3. _____
4. _____
5. _____
6. _____

# Thankful For...
MAKE A LIST OF 20 THINGS YOU ARE THANKFUL FOR TODAY

# Take Action
WHAT ARE 3 THINGS YOU CAN DO TO MOVE THINGS FORWARD?

1. _____
2. _____
3. _____

Date ___ / ___ / ___

# The Manifest List
WRITE DOWN SIX THINGS YOU'D LIKE TO MANIFEST IN YOUR LIFE

1. _____
2. _____
3. _____
4. _____
5. _____
6. _____

# Thankful For...
MAKE A LIST OF 20 THINGS YOU ARE THANKFUL FOR TODAY

# Take Action
WHAT ARE 3 THINGS YOU CAN DO TO MOVE THINGS FORWARD?

1. _____
2. _____
3. _____

Date    /   /

# Reflections

#TheManifestList

#TheManifestList

"Don't wish it was easier, wish you were better. Don't wish for less problems, wish for more skills. Don't wish for less challenges, wish for more wisdom. The major value in life is not what you get. The major value in life is what you become. Success is not to be pursued; it is to be attracted by the person you become."

- Jim Rohn

Here are some additional pages to reflect on how far come you have come and all that you've brought into your life...

Date     /     /

# Reflections

#TheManifestList

Date    /    /

# Reflections

#TheManifestList

Date     /     /

# Reflections

_____
_____
_____
_____
_____
_____
_____
_____
_____
_____
_____
_____
_____
_____
_____
_____

#TheManifestList

Date    /    /

# Reflections

#TheManifestList

Thank you for taking this journey with me.

I wish you all the success and love you desire.

#TheManifestList

**You can't achieve greatness without putting yourself out there.**

We will all make our mark on the world, one way or another. It may be small or big, negative or positive. The greater the impact, the greater the way we must show up.

#TheManifestList

## Connect with me:

www.ComplimentsOfSharon.com
Instagram: @SharonEGutierrez
Facebook: @ComplimentsOfSharon
Reorder at www.TheManifestList.com

Share your stories by tagging me or sending us a message online!

Made in United States
North Haven, CT
18 March 2022